AMOS

SEEK THE LORD AND LIVE

10 Publishing
a division of 10 of those.com

First published in Great Britain in 2018

British Library Cataloguing in Publication Data

A record for this book is available from the British Library

ISBN: 978-1-912373-17-8
Designed by Diane Warnes
Printed in the UK

10Publishing, a division of 10ofthose.com
Unit C, Tomlinson Road, Leyland, PR25 2DY, England
Email: info@10ofthose.com
Website: www.10ofthose.com

Matt Fuller

31 UNDATED DEVOTIONS THROUGH THE BOOK OF AMOS

DAY 1

READ Amos 1:1–2

If you go to a modern zoo, lions are one of the most impressive creatures to see. Normally they're lying around in the sun, not doing a lot. Yet if you get to see them tearing away at some raw meat with their enormous teeth, it's a magnificent sight.

However, if you somehow found yourself *inside* the enclosure with nothing between you and a hungry lion, then 'magnificent' might not be the thought running through your head. If an adult male lion shook its mane and let out a full-throated roar, then more likely it would be 'Uh-oh' or some more terrified equivalent that you would utter.

The book of Amos reveals the Living God as a roaring lion (v. 2), a picture that sets the tone of the book (also see 3:8). It's an uncomfortable image because He is roaring *against His own people*. Amos is a book designed to shake believers out of their moral complacency. Amos reminds us that the Lord is not a domestic cat who purrs when we bother to meet with Him; He is a lion who roars.

Even though it is placed third in the 'minor prophets', Amos was the first prophet of Israel who had his words written down in a book. 1:1 reveals that he was preaching around 760 BC to the northern kingdom of Israel. You can read what was going on at the time in 2 Kings 14:25–28. The headlines were that Israel had a popular monarch, Jeroboam II, who had ruled for nearly 40 years and brought great prosperity to them. They were wealthy and also one of the strongest military powers of the day. The people had every reason to feel comfortable with life. But they therefore neglected the Lord.

REFLECTION

Do you find that it's easy, when things are going well, to shrink God down to a convenient size for you?

DAY 2

READ Amos 1:3 – 2:3

Even though the Lord's complaint is against Israel, He starts off by proclaiming that He will judge every nation. God's throne was located in Jerusalem in the southern kingdom of Judah, but He's the sovereign ruler over *all the earth* and wants all to recognise that.

The repeated drumbeat is obvious when you read this passage:

- 'For three sins of ... even for four, I will not turn back my wrath'
- 'Because ...'
- 'I will send fire ... that will consume'

'For three ... even for four' probably is an equivalent expression to our 'this is the final straw'. The Lord is saying, 'Enough! The time has come for justice to fall.'

The sins of these pagan nations are what we would call 'crimes against humanity'. Damascus has 'threshed' humans (v. 3), that is dragged heavy iron rollers over people to crush them. Gaza 'took captive whole communities' and sold them as slaves (v. 6). You can almost imagine the screaming mother saying, 'Please leave the children.' Tyre and Edom are similarly culpable (vv. 9, 11). Ammon 'ripped open' pregnant women (v. 13), and so killed two people, merely 'to extend his borders.' Moab burned alive Edom's king (2:1).

Here is comfort the next time you see some horrific crime against humanity described on TV: the Lord sees; the Lord knows; the Lord will bring justice. That's an enormous relief.

REFLECTION

Praise God that He will judge all wickedness. The dictators of history who have died in luxury and comfort, having slaughtered thousands, will receive their punishment.

DAY 3

READ Amos 1:3 – 2:3

One of the striking features of God's blast of anger in chapters 1–2 is that none of the nations He denounced had God's Word. None of them had received the revelation of God that Israel had. Yet they are not being judged here for ignoring God or disobeying God's Word (unlike Israel – see day 4); they are judged for their mistreatment of others. As Paul explains in Romans 2:14–16, everyone should know in their conscience that this sort of behaviour is wrong.

That remains true of every individual. We may be a long, long way from committing war crimes, but all of us are still judged on how we treat others.

At the end of history, when people stand before Jesus for judgment, perhaps some might argue, 'It's not fair that I'm rejected. No one taught me the Ten Commandments, and no one told me about Jesus.' To this God could reply, 'Very well, I will judge you purely on how well you have kept the moral standards that you applied to everyone else.' Perhaps He might show footage of you saying, 'I hate it when people gossip, lie and are mean to others.' And then He may show further footage of you yourself gossiping, lying and being mean to others.

What is clear is that on that final day, the mouth of every person will be silent – for no one has consistently lived up to the standards they demand of others, let alone God's perfect law. That's true for us too. All of us do, say and think things of others that we know in our consciences are wrong. The Lord says repeatedly that He will not relent from judging people for their mistreatment of others.

REFLECTION

Confess the ways you've behaved in this way in the last week. Then praise God for the only person who had a pure conscience and treated others perfectly, Jesus, who nevertheless endured the 'unrelenting' judgment of God in our place.

DAY 4

READ Amos 2:4–16

Right up to 2:6 Israel would have been loving this sermon. All their pagan neighbours were being rebuked by God. Even their kinsmen in Judah were rebuked. Yet Amos' sermon has been building to his attack on Israel in 2:6–16. This is far longer and more detailed than the rebuke of any other nation.

The summary of their crimes comes in verses 6–8. In essence, they have oppressed the weakest in society. People are being sold into slavery (v. 6). Justice is denied to the poorest (v. 7). Father and son force themselves sexually upon the same slave girl, probably one who works for them (v. 7) and they are taking immorally gained products to church (v. 8).

It would be easy to think, '2:6–8 aren't great, but they are not as bad as the brutal pagans of chapter 1.' Yet the stress is that Israel should have known much better. They, like Judah (v. 4), knew the Lord and had received His grace. Israel was held to a higher standard because they should have understood better.

Similarly, I read recently of a 12-year-old girl who was sat in the family car waiting for the rest of her family. She put the key into the ignition to turn on the radio and listen to music. However, somehow she tragically put the car in reverse and ran over someone walking behind the car. That's heart-breaking, but the police treated it as an accident and not a crime. However, if a 30-year-old who has been driving for 12 years reversed over someone, it is treated as a criminal offence. The greater the knowledge, the more culpable you are.

REFLECTION

It's not good enough for a believer to say, for example, 'I may have sex when I shouldn't have done, but hey, I'm not a slave trader like them over there.' The Lord's comment is that in this way you 'profane my holy name' (v. 7). Are you conscious of dishonouring God's name before a watching world?

DAY 5

READ Amos 2:9–16

What makes Israel so guilty is not merely that they had received God's law, but that they had received His grace (vv. 9–12). 'Look what I did for you,' says the Lord in essence. With the repeated use of 'I …' He details how: I destroyed your enemies; I redeemed you from slavery; I guided you in the wilderness; I gave you a fertile land; I gave you godly leaders. It's not merely that I gave you knowledge, but that I showed you favour and kindness beyond all other nations. I showed you grace.

As God concludes, 'Is this not true, people of Israel?' (v. 11). *But* Israel's response was to get the Nazirites (young, keen, godly role models) drunk and to tell the Bible teachers to shut up (v. 12).

The Lord effectively says, 'I showed you grace and kindness when you had nothing and were desperate. If you truly understood that, you would treat others the same way, rather than exploiting the helpless.' Amos warned Israel that unless there was change, the whole nation – even the bravest and strongest – would be destroyed.

I can't tell you how to hear this word of Amos. Christians know that although we fail to honour the Lord rightly and we fail to treat others with the kindness God has sown us, we will not be punished. Christ was crushed in our place (v. 13). His strength failed Him as He died in order to give us life (v. 14). Although He was the bravest man to walk this planet, He was stripped naked (v. 16). So, the Lord will never destroy those who trust in Jesus. But He may well roar against some believers who mistreat others, despite receiving His grace.

Christians live somewhat in verses 9–12. We have received God's grace in Jesus. How are you responding?

REFLECTION

Do you need to hear the roar of the Lord warning you that you cannot claim to be a follower of Jesus and mistreat other people? We are those who know the Lord's kindness and generosity. We should pass that on.

DAY 6

READ Amos 3:1–2

Having declared God's imminent judgment upon Israel, Amos now spends chapters 3–6 trying to undermine their false sense of security. His audience would have thought it ridiculous that they would be invaded and destroyed. After all, they were wealthy, militarily strong and they had the Lord as their trump card 'in case of emergency'.

3:1–2 are a good summary of the shock of the book. They start so well! Israel has been adopted as God's family (v. 1). They've been redeemed from slavery (v. 1). They've been chosen above the other nations (v. 2). But the second half of verse 2 is shocking: 'therefore I will punish you for all your sins.' God will not have spoiled children in His family.

Likewise, sometimes the individual Christian might declare, 'I've been adopted into God's family. I've been redeemed from slavery to sin and Satan. I've been chosen for holiness.' But if we show no sign of living by the family rules, after a while we can't really call ourselves Christians. Jesus warned, 'Not everyone who says to me, "Lord, Lord," will enter the kingdom of heaven, but only the one who does the will of my Father who is in heaven ... everyone who hears these words of mine and does not put them into practice is like a foolish man who built his house on sand' (Matt 7:21, 26).

Amos wants to warn us of presumption. Just being part of a church and claiming the name Christian is not enough. The Lord wants His children to live like members of His family.

REFLECTION

How do the privileges of being a Christian affect you? What difference does it make to be able to call God 'Father'? Are you encouraged by seeing yourself increasingly displaying a family likeness to Jesus?

DAY 7

READ Read Amos 3:1–8

This section of Amos divides into three 'judgment oracles'. Three times Israel is told, 'Hear this word ...' (3:1; 4:1; 5:1).

One difficulty with applying the book of Amos is that the nation of Israel was both a political body (a nation) and a spiritual body (the people of God). This side of the cross, the church is only a spiritual body as the people of God. We are not a political nation. So we'll have to work hard at some of the social and political comments Amos makes.

By way of introduction:

THE NATION OF ISRAEL

Could never lose God's covenant promises completely (9:8–9).

Could lose the blessings of the covenant in life (lose the land; lose crops; be invaded).

Israel was mixed – some individuals were true believers; others were not. Amos is preaching so that even though judgment is coming, there may be a remnant of true Israelites who would remain faithful.

THE CHRISTIAN CHURCH

Can never be defeated or overcome.

Can lose the blessings of salvation in this life (Heb. 12:6). God may discipline a church or an individual to bring them to repentance.

The church is mixed – some are true believers; others are self-deceived (Matt. 7:21–23). Even in gospel churches there are those who were never truly converted and will fall away, and those who are faithful.

In 3:3–8 Amos adopts a little series of riddles. The answers are clearly: no (v. 3); no, no (v. 4 – lions don't reveal themselves needlessly); no, no (v. 5). Then the shift comes in verse 6 where the response is yes. Yes, people do tremble when a trumpet warns them of attack. And yes, disaster comes because the Lord calls it. In verses 7–8 Amos declares that he cannot hold back from warning the people of God's judgment now that it has been revealed.

REFLECTION

What about you? Did Jesus warn of God's judgment? Yes. Did He die so that whoever believes in Him may not perish but have eternal life? Yes. Have you spoken of this to others?

DAY 8

READ Amos 3:9–12

Amos attacks two deceptive sources of security in the remainder of the chapter: wealth (vv. 9–12), which we will look at today, and worship (vv. 13–15).

Clearly the people were impressed with fortresses (vv. 9–11). The scholars tell us that these were fortified luxury houses. We might compare them to modern big houses hidden behind security gates.

Strangely it is the fortresses of Ashdod and Egypt that are summoned as witnesses (v. 9). These pagan nations are to observe Israel's unrest, oppression and, in a shocking phrase, that: 'They do not know how to do right' (v. 10). Israel has lost all sense of moral bearing. Nor do the Israelites worry about the future, because the affluent have their fortresses. But Amos tells them they may store up wealth in their fortresses; but they'll be plundered and looted (v. 10).

Not a lot will be left of Israel. The picture in verse 12 comes from Exodus 22. If you were a shepherd and a wild animal ate one of your master's sheep, then you had to take back a piece of bone to prove that you hadn't stolen the animal. God says that a few Israelites will be saved when the land is invaded, but not a lot. All that will be left of the fortresses is a bedstead or a piece of fabric from a sofa.

So for us, do we perhaps think that our future is secure because we own a house? Or because we have some money in the bank? Or because the bank of mum and dad will bail us out?

Do you think these things make you safe? The Lord says that He can take away them all.

REFLECTION

What makes you feel safe? Do you feel safer when you look to the Lord or when you look at your bank balance or possessions?

DAY 9

READ Amos 3:13 – 4:5

The issue is still false security. Israel trusted in its wealth and its worship. Let's focus on their worship today. Around 930 BC the kingdom of Solomon had split. Rehoboam became king of the two tribes of Judah, where Jerusalem was located. Jeroboam I became king of the ten northern tribes of Israel. Jeroboam I was a bit nervous that his citizens would keep going back to the temple of Jerusalem. His solution was to create two golden calves and place them at Bethel and Dan (1 Kgs. 12). He effectively declared, 'Here you go, Israel. There's no need to go to Jerusalem like God told you to. I've made it far more convenient for you to knock God off the "to-do list". You can pop in and doff your cap at Bethel or Dan. A choice of two places! Brilliant, hey?'

The people thought that if they grasped hold of the horns of the altar upon which the calves stood, then all their sins would be forgiven. But the Lord warns, 'the horns of the altar will be cut off and fall to the ground' (v. 14). Their false sense of forgiveness will be destroyed. We are meant to worship the Lord on His terms, not in a manner which is convenient to us and fits around our lives.

Then in 4:4–5 the Lord opts for outright sarcasm. You need to read these verses with that tone: 'Why don't you go to Bethel and sin!' They are told to go through the motions of religious worship. The sting is in the end of verse 5: they brag and boast about their worship 'for this is what you love to do'. They're not there to worship God; they're only going to make themselves feel good.

REFLECTION

Although our motives are always mixed, do we go to church to honour the Lord, hear from Him and encourage others? Or do we go because it makes us feel good? Is it 'what we love to do'?

DAY 10

READ Amos 4:1–3

Ouch. I can't remember a preacher ever turning to the congregation and saying, 'Hear this, you fat cows!' Amos was not a man for genteel company. Here he attacks the affluent women of society. To be clear, he is not criticising them merely for being wealthy. Rather he attacks them for how they obtained their wealth. It is due to the oppression of the poor and the crushing of the needy. Their wealth comes at the expense of others. There is clearly a sense of entitlement here as the women turn to their husbands and in effect demand, 'Bring me another gin and tonic, darling.'

The Lord warns them that there will be a complete reversal. They who live in luxury will be pulled away with hooks through holes in the city wall. It will be miserable.

It's helpful to know that the cows of Bashan were actually prized beasts. In that culture this was the finest cow there was – it was top of the range. So it seems that Amos' point is that here are a bunch of women who cared only about their bodies and not about their souls. They may have been 'top animals', but they still had the values of cows.

It makes us ask some awkward questions:

- Do we care obsessively about our body to the neglect of our soul?
- Are we content to expand our own wealth without a thought to how the most vulnerable in society are surviving?

I'm writing this a couple of weeks after the Grenfell tower went up in flames, killing dozens of people in Kensington, London. That second question feels quite awkward and acute for many in our affluent capital city. Having more money can give you more choices in life, but it cannot nurture or protect your soul.

REFLECTION

Have you recently heeded Jesus warning about the deceitfulness of wealth (Matt. 13:22)? It can choke the Word of God so that it bears no fruit in your life. It offers a deceptive security.

DAY 11

READ Amos 4:6–11

Here is a staggering list of ways that the Lord has blocked Israel and caused them difficulty. There were five ways in which He had sought to discipline them and shock them into returning to Him, but they did not. We need to know that the Lord will allow His people to suffer pain and hardship as a warning in order that they may return to Him and ultimately be safe.

I read an article a while ago about a lad called Stephen Pete. He has a genetic disease which means he feels no pain. He described how as a child of five months he bit through his tongue and how he badly burnt himself. He spent most of his childhood with a cast on as he pushed his body beyond a point where most of us would say, 'Ow,' and stop. He described being at a skate rink and having a good time until someone pointed out that his trousers were covered with blood and that he was skating on a broken leg. He titled the article: 'The agony of feeling no pain'.

In life, physical pain is a warning to us so that we don't experience the agony of serious harm. The Lord tells His people that He will send upon them the pain of no food, no crops and no rain so that they don't experience the pain of something far worse: His decisive judgment.

You and I need to be cautious. In the Bible pain and suffering are not always discipline. Job's pain was not. Jesus' suffering was not. But when God sends troubles, it is sensible to ask the question, 'Lord, is there something of which I need to repent? Do I need to return to you in some way?'

REFLECTION

Are you willing to view hardships in your life as the Lord's discipline? Hebrews 12:4–11 tells us that His discipline is a mark of His love. He wants us to return to Him and keep going walking with Him.

DAY 12

READ Amos 4:6–13

Verses 12 and 13 conclude the first two judgment oracles beginning 'Hear this …' (3:1 and 4:1). The Lord has said that Israel placed their security in their fortresses of wealth (3:9–12) and in their self-centred worship (4:4–5). They have also ignored God's warnings. 'Therefore this is what I will do …' declares God (v. 12).

The 'this' is a reference back to 3:11 and the fact that Israel would be invaded by Assyria. This did indeed happen, leading to Israel's destruction in 722 BC.

At this conclusion the Lord emphasises His mastery over all creation. It's what He does repeatedly throughout the book of Amos. It's as if He is saying, 'You do realise that I am the creator God who controls all the elements? You do realise that you are tiny creatures and I am the Almighty one?' Here and another eight times in the book He describes Himself as the LORD God of Armies (3:13; 4:13; 5:14–15, 16, 27; 6:8, 14; 9:5). It may be translated as 'LORD God Almighty' or 'LORD, the God of hosts', but it has a military tone. You cannot resist Him.

Back in yesterday's section, it was almost as if the Lord had turned the events of the Exodus against the Israelites: they would experience famine (vv. 6–7); locusts (v. 9), plagues, (v. 10) and destruction (v. 11). Here in verse 13 it is a plague of darkness.

We are foolish to think that we are anything more than little creatures. It is madness to resist the Almighty Creator who is God of Armies and can send the power of creation against us.

And yet … there is a hint of hope in 4:12: 'prepare to meet your God'. Israel may have abused and neglected their relationship with the Lord, but He still calls Himself 'your' God. Return to Him while there is time!

REFLECTION

How often do you reflect upon the overwhelming power of the Lord? It's easy to blame, ignore or shrink down the Lord. Take time to meditate upon His overwhelming power.

DAY 13

READ Amos 5:1–3

Amos 5:1 begins the third judgment oracle: 'Hear this ...' Yet this one begins very differently in tone. It has neither the fierce anger of 3:1–3 nor the biting sarcasm of 4:4–5. Rather here is the Lord lamenting over the judgment that must fall upon Israel. We should imagine 5:1–2 being read out to the soundtrack from *Schindler's List* – a sad, lonely violin plays in the background. It's so sad that young 'virgin' Israel, with her whole life ahead of her, is about to fall. She will never rise again and there is no one to lift her up. Not even the Lord will help. Verse 3 reveals that she will be literally decimated. It's a tragic scenario and one the Lord laments.

A while back I read of Judge Phillip Wassall. He presided in the trial of a lorry driver who had killed a motorcyclist when he carried out a dangerous U-turn. The judge sentenced the driver to four years in prison for 'death by dangerous driving', but as he did so he broke down in tears. He said, 'I cry chiefly for the two young girls who have been robbed of their father who was killed. Yet I cry also for the stupidity of this lorry driver who has ruined his own life too.'

That is a faint echo of our perfect God. He is perfect in His justice, but not dispassionate. He laments over the judgment that must fall. Elsewhere we're told that judgment is God's 'strange work', His 'alien task' (Is. 28:21) and that He takes no pleasure in the death of the wicked (Ezek. 33:11; see also 18:23). We must hold together His overwhelming power in justice with His compassion and love for those He has made. We praise Him for the cross!

REFLECTION

Do you have the same sense of compassion as the Lord? When you look at the sin of people around you and the corruption of your town, village or city, do you rush to condemn or do you cry over the fate of the lost?

DAY 14

READ Amos 5:1–17

When you read all of chapter five, it's quite hard to make sense of it. It's almost as if someone has chopped up three different speeches and then jumbled them together. There is the certainty of unavoidable judgment, followed by an appeal for repentance. I take it that the writer wants to unsettle us and make us feel like we're on the deck of a ship swaying violently in a storm.

I think that the structure works like this:

Lament (vv. 1–3)
  Offer of mercy (vv. 4–6)
    Accusation of injustice (v. 7)
      Hymn of God's power (vv. 8–9)
    Accusation of injustice (vv. 10–13)
  Offer of mercy (vv. 14–15)
Lament (vv. 16–17)

How can God declare that judgment is certain in 5:1–3, but then immediately call Israel to repent and seek Him in 5:4–6? It's a tension that grows throughout the book, becoming clearest in 9:8. The answer is that although the majority of Israel would be destroyed, there would be a remnant who were truly believers and so did indeed seek Him in repentance. As 5:15 states, 'Perhaps the LORD God Almighty will have mercy on the remnant'.

This concept of the remnant became clearer in the later prophets, especially Isaiah and Jeremiah (see Is. 10). Paul picks up on this in Romans 11:5: 'So too, at the present time there is a remnant chosen by grace.' God never abandoned His promise to Israel, but only a remnant has trusted Him.

So, overall the book of Amos is the record of God pronouncing judgment *with the aim* that a remnant would repent and truly trust in the Lord. They would truly seek Him rather than engage in superficial religious activity such as a pilgrimage to Bethel, Gilgal or Beersheba (5:5). True preaching always has that divisive impact.

REFLECTION

What do you think it means to truly seek the Lord as opposed to being engaged in religious activity?

How do the parallel verses of 5:14–15 help explain what it means to seek the Lord?

DAY 15

READ Amos 5:7–13

Let's turn to the issue of justice which so heavily concerns the book of Amos. 5:7 is the first time that Amos explicitly condemns Israel for abandoning justice and righteousness (*mishpat* and *tsedeq* in the original Hebrew; see also 5:24; 6:12). In fact, it's worse than that. As the ESV translates verse 7, some have turned 'justice into wormwood', a highly bitter herb synonymous with bitter calamity. Righteousness has been dramatically cast to the ground. The two words have overlapping meanings yet justice has a little more sense of righting individual wrongs – it is the judge who ensures that someone is granted justice. Righteousness has a little more of a communal sense – it is justice within a whole community or society.

Within His Word, God reveals Himself as One with a particular concern for the oppressed or marginalised. More than 50 times He insists upon care for the fatherless, widow and alien. These were the powerless with no one to provide for them or protect them.

To desire to see a church and a society where there is righteousness and justice for all is to have the heart of God. To be indifferent to such issues is to fall well short of Christlikeness. As an example, my church is located in an area of London which is synonymous with prostitution. There are huge numbers of women who have been illegally trafficked for the sex trade. We could all say, 'That's not my problem – I don't visit prostitutes.' Yet a number are involved in reaching out to these young girls, working with the police to try and see them rescued out of slavery while also seeking to share the gospel with them. I hope that Amos would approve.

REFLECTION

Do you tend to view righteousness only in personal terms? Do you look for communal righteousness in a church and a church without favouritism? Do you care about a just society?

DAY 16

READ Amos 5:10–13

Here are further details on the lack of justice. First, there was double taxation on those who could least afford it to pay for the luxuries of the elite (v. 11). Second, it seems that there was no guarantee of impartial justice in the courts (vv. 10, 12). Those of us who live in countries that operate under the rule of law and whose legal system is overwhelmingly free from corruption should give thanks to God. It's a blessing that not all nations have!

I want to pause and briefly ask how does a pursuit of justice in this world relate to the task of evangelism? It's an important question and there's probably a drift in every generation towards social justice projects. The watching world will be positive about Christians when they're involved in anti-trafficking campaigns and often negative when they share the gospel. It's always nice to be liked! So how do we hold biblically to both with an appropriate emphasis on eternity?

These words of John Piper's from the Lausanne conference in 2010 are a helpful starting point:

Could the evangelical church say – we Christians care about all suffering, especially eternal suffering? I hope we can say that. But if we feel resistant to saying 'especially eternal suffering,' or if we feel resistant to saying 'we care about all suffering in this age,' then either we have a defective view of hell or a defective heart.

Believers who are like Christ care for justice in this world, but they care for people's eternal souls even more. As Christians we should care first for justice within the church and then secondly for justice in the wider world, remembering that the Lord is sovereign over the pagan nations too (chapter 1) and cares about their societies.

REFLECTION

Are you in danger of being too obsessed with pursuing social justice in this life or do you lean towards indifference to the plight of the widow, orphan and alien?

DAY 17

READ Amos 5:14–15

In chapter five, 'Seek [the LORD] and live' (v. 4) is paralleled with 'Seek good, not evil, that you may live' (v. 14). It seems very similar to Christ's command to His disciples: 'remain in my love' (John 15:9 10). What is the evidence of remaining in Christ's love? It's loving one another (John 15:12). And the power to live this way? It's knowing that Christ has loved us sacrificially (John 15:13).

Obedience does not merit or bring us into God's love – that is always an act of His grace. Yet our obedience is the evidence of our love for Jesus. It is in expression of our faith.

In Amos 5, the evidence that we are seeking the Lord is that we seek good not evil. In fact, it's more than our actions; it's that we 'hate evil' and 'love good' (v. 15). Amos doesn't call for a veneer of moral action; he wants a love of good and hatred of evil to be the disposition of the heart. Our external action flows from our internal emotions. So how do we encourage a love of justice within ourselves? We remember God's work for us.

Back in Deuteronomy 15:15, the LORD said, 'Remember that you were slaves in Egypt and the LORD your God redeemed you; that is why I give you this command today.' One example of this was that they were to freely lend to the poor and needy (Deut. 15:14).

In Ephesians 2:12, Paul describes Christians as being 'excluded from citizenship ... without hope and without God'. *But* Jesus Christ showed us mercy and grace when we had nothing. Christians know that, spiritually speaking, we were orphans, widows, aliens. We were enslaved by sin. Yet when we had nothing and deserved nothing, Christ sought us out and showed us generous love and grace.

Knowing that empowers us to go and give of ourselves for others who are marginalised, excluded and without hope – first in the church and then in the world.

REFLECTION

When you look at injustice in the world, do you hate it? Do you love justice? Does meditating upon Christ's generosity to you when you were excluded help you show a similar concern for others?

DAY 18

READ Amos 5:18–27

Let me remind you that in chapters 3–6 Amos is trying to persuade Israel that they are not safe. They may think that a booming economy and dominant military protect them, but within a generation they were to be invaded by Assyria and destroyed. So after the three 'Hear this …' oracles, we now have two 'Woe to you …' prophecies in 5:18 and 6:1. In the first Amos attacks the idea that religion can protect them. In the second he undermines again their confidence in wealth. Both 'Woes' end with warnings: of exile (5:27) and of invasion (6:14).

Today we will focus on verse 18–20. Evidently Israel had misunderstood the Day of the Lord. Israel expected a Day when the Lord would judge how everyone had lived and reward or penalise them accordingly. Israel assumed that, as a nation, the Day would be great for them – they would be rewarded and all their enemies destroyed. But Amos warns it will be a day of darkness, not light. Verses 19–20 describe a man desperately fleeing from one danger to another. The Day of the Lord was going to be a day of pitch dark, without a ray of brightness. Frightening. Terrifying. That Day came for Israel in 722 BC.

The Bible is clear that history is heading towards one more final Day. On the Day when Jesus will return and judge the world, no one will be worthy of reward; everyone who has lived will deserve judgment – except one man: Jesus Christ.

Yet God in His kindness has set in history two days of darkness that matter for you and me. One is the Day of Judgment, but the first was the day of the cross. The day that Jesus died, a surprising darkness fell over the land between midday and 3 p.m. It became a day of darkness, not light, when God's judgment on all the sins of those trusting in Christ fell instead on Jesus.

REFLECTION

What will the Day of the Lord look like for you? We either trust that the darkness of judgment fell upon Jesus in our place or we will face it ourselves. Give thanks for the day of the cross!

DAY 19

READ Amos 5:21–27

Does God like your church meetings? He didn't like those in Israel: 'I hate ... I despise ... I will not accept ... I will have no regard for ... I will not listen to ...' I expect that this Sunday there will be church services up and down the land that God will hate. They will stink offensively to Him (v. 21).

They may well be church leaders breaking bread earnestly while God says, 'I hate that.' There may be crowds of 1000s swaying intensely as they sing songs while God says, 'I hate that.' There may be preachers delivering impeccably crafted sermons which people diligently transcribe while God says, 'I hate that.' Note that it is not that God hates all gatherings, but that these features demonstrated something that was wrong in Israel. He said to the Israelites that He hated 'your' festivals, assemblies, songs, harps. There was something about Israel that made their 'worship' obnoxious. The lacking element is revealed again in verse 24: their religion did not affect their behaviour.

It's a beautiful picture in verse 24, famously used by Martin Luther King. Justice is not meant to be something that you turn your mind to for one hour a week. It is meant to be continuous, always rolling, never fading.

In a brief history lesson in verses 25–26, the Lord reminds the Israelites of their 40 years in the wilderness. This text is a little tricky but Amos implies that they had not only offered sacrifices; there was a concern for justice then too (much as in v. 24). But now they merely worship convenient gods of their making.

For us today, what is religion that the Lord finds acceptable? James 1:26–27 tells us, 'Those who consider themselves religious and yet do not keep a tight rein on their tongues deceive themselves, and their religion is worthless. Religion that God our Father accepts as pure and faultless is this: to look after orphans and widows in their distress and to keep oneself from being polluted by the world.'

REFLECTION

What do your church gatherings look like? Do they produce justice that rolls like a river? Does your religion have a concern for the powerless?

DAY 20

READ Amos 6:1–14

Here Amos attacks the complacency of the wealthy. It is clear that it is the leaders of society, the 'notable men', who take his hardest hit (v. 1). The problem is not that they are wealthy but that they don't care about injustice and that they proudly think that they're secure.

Amos quotes these elite men in verse 2. They are telling the people to compare themselves to other poorer nations. That's always a good way to boost your self-esteem!

Amos then attacks them for their uncaring wealth in verses 4–6. They lie in opulence, eat only the finest foods and think that the songs they write are as good as David's! They may enjoy luxury and drink wine not from glasses but bowls! *But* they don't grieve over the ruin of the nation (v. 6). Once again they are told that they turn justice and righteousness into poison and bitterness (v. 12).

The Lord hates their smug sense of security in their own resources (v. 8). It will not save them from God's judgment (vv. 9–10).

Here is a word primarily for those who exercise power in this world. You will be held to account by the Lord for your indifference to those who are poorest. Crucially nor can your wealth protect you!

I read recently that a number of Californian tech billionaires are buying up land in remote parts of New Zealand to flee to in the case of a nuclear holocaust. Well, good luck in outrunning a nuclear missile! It seems such a silly plan. Yet, do you ever find yourself thinking, 'I need more money in the bank to be secure. If I had one month's savings in the bank, I'd feel safer ... If I had one year's savings ... Phew, I have the bank of mum and dad to fall back on'?

REFLECTION

What is your confidence in? Verse 8 reminds us that the only place of security is the Lord.

DAY 21

READ Amos 7:1 – 8:3

Having spent four chapters trying to persuade the Israelites that their complacency is misplaced, Amos now spends the last three chapters on five visions of the coming judgment. The first four are in pairs:

7:1–3 The swarm of locusts

7:4–6 The judgment of fire

Both are warnings of total devastation. But Amos pleads for mercy and the Lord relents.

7:7–9 The plumb line

8:1–3 A basket of ripe fruit

These are less catastrophic and suggest a careful judgment being made. There is no pleading. The Lord waits 'no longer'.

9:1–4 The final judgment

There is no pair because this is the end.

At this point in the book, around 760 BC, God's patience with Israel runs out. We understand in normal life that patience is a wonderful virtue, but unlimited patience is not. A good parent is patient with a misbehaving child, yet eventually there will be some form of correction. Otherwise the parent is just lazy or indifferent.

We also need to remember the purpose of God's patience. As Romans 2:4 teaches us, '... do you show contempt for the riches of his kindness, forbearance and patience, not realising that God's kindness is intended to lead you to repentance?'

REFLECTION

Who are the unbelievers you love and make you grateful that the Lord has been patient thus far? Pray that they come to repentance. We do not know when His patience will end.

DAY 22

READ Amos 7:1–6

Twice here we're told that 'the Lord relented' (vv. 3, 6). It's a Hebrew word that is also translated as 'repented' or 'changed his mind'. How do we understand that when elsewhere we're told, 'He who is the Glory of Israel does not lie or change his mind; for he is not a human being, that he should change his mind' (1 Sam. 15:29)? There are three things to notice:

1. Amos' pleading is prompted by God. In both visions the Lord adopts the tactic of 'leaking news' to Amos to produce a response. The Lord 'showed' these events to Amos (vv. 1, 4). The Lord *wants* Amos to plead.
2. There's a desperate intensity to Amos' appeal. He 'cried out' and begged the Lord to stop (vv. 2, 5). Biblical prayers always have such an intensity for the lost. When Jesus approached Jerusalem and saw the city, He wept over it and its wretched future (Luke 19:41). When Paul considered the plight of his fellow Jews, he declared, 'I have great sorrow and unceasing anguish in my heart ... my heart's desire and prayer to God for the Israelites is that they may be saved (Rom. 9:2; 10:1).
3. Amos' plea is answered by our *Personal God*. The Lord relates to us in our time. He is not a distant, uncaring deity, such as the concept of Allah. In verses 3 and 5 the Lord relented *as He had always intended to do*. God prompted Amos to pray so that He could have mercy in response to those prayers. The Lord reveals Himself as personal and responsive to the prayers of His people. Martin Luther famously wrote to his barber, 'Prayer is not overcoming God's reluctance, but laying hold of his willingness.'

Pleading for others releases God's mercy. That's what the Lord intends. So what stops us? Busyness? Fatalism: 'It won't make a difference'? Lack of compassion? God have mercy on us.

REFLECTION

What stops you from pleading for the Lord to have mercy on others? Ask Him for a heart like Amos, Paul or Jesus and plead!

DAY 23

READ Amos 7:1–6

We considered yesterday that we should plead for God to have mercy on others. This is true. Yet it's impossible to read of this incident without thinking of the One who pleads for us:

... because Jesus lives for ever, he has a permanent priesthood. Therefore he is able to save completely those who come to God through him, because he always lives to intercede *for them (Heb. 7:24–25, my emphasis).*

Who then is the one who condemns? No one. Christ Jesus who died – more than that, who was raised to life – is at the right hand of God and is also interceding *for us (Rom. 8:34, my emphasis).*

Jesus may well plead, 'Lord forgive my people. They are so small and pathetic.' Yet, His pleading is not merely hopeful, like Amos'. It is confident and certain. It is pleading on the basis of His perfect life of obedience and a death that has paid for all of our sin. Jesus does not *simply* plead for mercy; He can also plead for justice – we cannot be punished as punishment has already fallen upon Him. Nor can God's patience with us in our ongoing struggles with sin ever run out because Jesus lives and pleads forever on the basis of His perfect life and substitutionary death.

For more than 150 years Christians have delighted to sing of this truth:

Before the throne of God above
I have a strong, a perfect plea:
A great High Priest, whose name is love
Who ever lives and pleads for me.
My name is written on his hands,
My name is hidden in his heart;
I know that while in heaven he stands
No power can force me to depart,
No power can force me to depart.[1]

REFLECTION

No matter what we've done this day, or this week, we have utter confidence of the Lord's love for us because Jesus is pleading on our behalf. Look up and give thanks for your interceding High Priest.

[1] Charitie Lees Bancroft, 'Before the throne of God above'.

DAY 24

READ Amos 7:7 – 8:3

The picture of a plumb line summons up the image of God measuring Israel against the plumb line of His Word. A plumb line reveals faults that we might miss at a superficial glance. It shows us that the wallpaper or shelves may be wonky. The Lord has measured Israel and found her morally warped.

Why does God relent in the first two visions but not after the next two? Why does His patience run out in 7:7–9 and 8:1–3 so that He declares, 'I will spare them no longer' (7:8; 8:2)? The answer comes in Amos' conflict with the high priest Amaziah. This incident is deliberately placed between visions 3 and 4 to explain why God's patience has ended. We'll look at some of the details tomorrow, but the headline is that this final rejection of God's Word by the leadership of Israel leads to the final rejection of Israel by God.

Amaziah is the chief priest in the land and in verse 10 he declares that the nation cannot bear the Word of God. He appeals to the monarch, Jeroboam II, in verses 10–11. I presume there's a gap in time while they await the response. That appears to have come by verse 12 for Amaziah tells Amos to get out of the land: there'll be no more preaching or prophesying here. In other words, by this stage the government and the church both say, 'We've had enough of the Word of God. We don't like what it says and we're not listening.'

At this point, the Lord effectively says, 'Enough. I will spare them no longer. I've been patient with your superficial worship. I've been patient with your immorality. I've been patient with your disregard for justice. But now you are deliberately refusing to listen to my Word. Enough.'

REFLECTION

Can you think of churches or denominations that have drifted from the plumb line of God's Word?

History reveals that eventually the Lord says, 'Enough', and they shrink away to nothing.

DAY 25

READ Amos 7:10–17

It's a highly personal conflict between Amos and Amaziah. God's man is placed under enormous pressure.

He is subjected to misrepresentation (v. 11), as Amaziah exaggerates the words that Amos had spoken, telling the king that 'Amos is raising a conspiracy against you' (v. 10).

He is exposed to temptation (v. 12). The priest tells Amos that he would have a far easier life back in the nation of Judah.

He is treated to intimidation (v. 13). In essence Amaziah is declaring, 'Do you know where you are, Amos? This is the king's sanctuary and the temple of the Lord. Who are you to stand up to us in this place?!'

Yet Amos' response is a great encouragement to us. In verse 14 he effectively says, 'I don't get paid for this, you know. This is not how I earn my living. I have a perfectly well-paid job back in Judah, but I'm using my holiday allowance to come here and warn you. God told me to come and preach here and so I have. Oh and by the way, here's God's Word to you personally in verse 17.'

We may find this last verse a shock, but it's a reminder that those who claim to speak for the Lord are held to a higher standard: 'Not many of you should become teachers ... because you know that we who teach will be judged more strictly' (Jas. 3:1).

Amos is a great model for many of us. The Lord does not always call people from their present line of work in order that they might deliver God's warning of judgment, but God does call all of us, shepherds and fig cultivators and school teachers and taxi drivers and decorators and lawyers, to tell people about Jesus where he has placed us.

REFLECTION

Ask the Lord to give you courage to keep speaking of Jesus, even when you are misrepresented, tempted for a quiet life and intimidated by influential figures.

DAY 26

READ Amos 8:4–10

After the fourth vision there's an interlude (8:4–14) before the fifth vision comes in chapter 9. It serves to build tension, but also returns to one of the dominant themes of the book: injustice.

The slight shift here is that Amos is not attacking the elites of society but the merchants. He accuses them of wanting to 'do away with the poor' (v. 4) – a kind of social cleansing. He quotes them in verses 5–6, revealing that they sit in church longing for the service to be over so they can get back to earning money unscrupulously in order to turn the poorest of society into their slaves.

Does that still happen in the modern West? Certainly some London borough councils are accused of replacing social housing with more expensive private property and then rehousing their tenants outside of London. Social cleansing still takes place.

We may not trouble ourselves with such things, but God does: 'I will never forget anything they have done' (v. 7). It's as if God gets out His highlighter pen when He says, 'The LORD has sworn by himself'. What wonderful comfort to those who receive no justice in this life. God will never forget anything the wicked have unjustly done.

Verses 8–10 describe the judgment that fell upon Israel in 722 BC. Yet for us now it is also evocative of Good Friday:

- A day when people gathered for the religious festival of Passover
- A day when darkness darkened the earth as the sun went down at noon (v. 9)
- A day when the ground split open as Christ died, much like the land trembling (v. 8)
- A day when God the Father mourned His only Son (v. 10)

Again we are faced with choosing a day of darkness – either trusting in the cross or facing the darkness of judgment when Christ returns: a day when God will not forget any injustice done.

REFLECTION

How does the knowledge that God will never forget injustices help you to bear with injustice now, either against you personally or on a larger scale?

DAY 27

READ Amos 8:11–14

Here a different sort of judgment is described. It seems to be describing events after the calamitous judgment upon Israel depicted in 8:7–10. When people have lost everything and there is nowhere else to turn, then they will attempt to seek God's Word (v. 12) – yet in vain.

It's not that all the Bibles have been stolen, but rather there will be 'a famine of hearing the words of the LORD' (v. 11). There will be no faithful preachers. God's judgment upon a nation who had rejected His Word is that He will withdraw faithful preaching.

The young (v. 13) are particularly highlighted as being vulnerable as a result. This may be emphasising that *even* the strongest in the nation will faint and fall. Yet I wonder if there's also an element of gullibility. When there's a famine of the Word of God, the vacuum normally gets filled by other forms of religion or spirituality. Young people are perhaps particularly susceptible to trying new things and seeking out new experiences and adventures (that's generally a strength and a weakness). Here the young are prepared to 'swear by the sin of Samaria' – probably a reference to the pagan god worshipped before Israel arrived (2 Kgs. 17:30–33). Some worshipped the golden calf at Dan if they wanted physical, tangible religion they could see and touch.

Although it seems likely that this passage follows on in time from 8:8–10, the fact that Amos describes 'days' in verse 11 rather than 'the Day' hints that perhaps this can happen at other times in history. It's certainly the case that up and down our land there seem to be many churches where there is a famine of hearing the Words of God faithfully proclaimed.

REFLECTION

Do you cherish the preaching of God's Word, when you hear the Words of the Lord? If you take it for granted, can you see how devastating it would be if the Lord sent a famine of it?

DAY 28

READ Amos 9:1–10

This is the fifth and final vision of the book and the stress is on no escape. God declares explicitly, 'Not one will get away, none will escape' (v. 1). You can try digging down to the depths of the earth or you can try climbing up to the highest heavens (v. 2). You could try hiding on Carmel, the highest mountain of the region, or you could try hiding at the bottom of the sea (v. 3). The outcome remains: no escape.

Once again we're given an overwhelming image of the Lord of creation in verses 5–6. He only has to touch the earth for it to melt. The Israelites cannot evade Him. Indeed, in verse 7 God now views them as no different to the Cushites or Ethiopians. God is saying that their behaviour is so miserable that they have become nothing more to Him than any other nation.

Yet still there remains hope for some. There will be a remnant of Israel (see day 14) who pass through God's sieve (v. 9) and are safe.

Those who sought the Lord and said, 'We find our security in you, not in ourselves and Mount Samaria' (in contrast to those in 6:1) are saved. Those who said, 'Disaster will not overtake or meet us' (v. 10) will face the sword of judgment.

This is devastating and yet I can't help read verses 2–4 without thinking of the difference it makes to believe in Christ. There should have been no possibility of any of us escaping from God's judgment. Now, in Him, there is no possibility of losing His love: 'For I am convinced that neither death nor life, neither angels nor demons, neither the present nor the future, nor any powers, neither height nor depth, nor anything else in creation, will be able to separate us from the love of God that is in Christ Jesus our Lord' (Rom. 8:38–39).

REFLECTION

How does viewing the Lord as One who melts the earth with His touch and One who lets no sinner escape cause you to give greater thanks for the One who did not escape the wrath of God on the cross?

DAY 29

READ Amos 9:11–15

What a change of mood in these last five verses! This is clearly not the same Day of Judgment that Amos has spoken about for most of the book. It is a day of hope. It may be helpful to list some of the different ways those of us living this side of the cross understand the Day of the LORD when reading an Old Testament prophet:

NEAR FUTURE

Day of judgment inflicted on Judah by Assyria (722 BC).

HOPEFUL FUTURE

Judah's return from exile (539 BC).

FAR FUTURE

Cross as the Day of Darkness (AD 33), after which nations bear God's name in the church so that people from every tribe and nation become Christians.

FAR HOPEFUL FUTURE

We will be planted in the New Creation, never to be uprooted.

These five verses actually contain two promises. In verses 11–12, the Lord promises to restore His people. There's a sense in which this has been the whole purpose of the book of Amos. The Lord warned Israel of destruction *so that* through this there might emerge a people genuinely trusting in Him. When the book of Amos was read by the neighbouring nation of Judah in the years following 722 BC, the purpose would have been the same: to produce a people trusting in the Lord. That purpose remains for us.

These two verses are quoted in the New Testament, at the council of Jerusalem in Acts 15:16–17, when the disciples discuss the terms on which Gentiles could enter the church. James cites them to say that the tent or shelter of King David was being repaired by the greater David, Jesus Christ. Here is a prediction that Gentiles would join the church equally with Jews through faith in Jesus. People of all nations would bear the name of Jesus.

REFLECTION

Have you had the great privilege of meeting with Christians from very different cultures and nations? It's a wonderful blessing that, although we may appear very different, we are united in the one Saviour. What a joy that is.

DAY 30

READ Amos 9:13–15

What a magnificent picture. The Lord promises to renew His creation in the future. Here is a depiction of the New Creation that God will create when Christ returns. Amos takes the language of blessing from Deuteronomy 28 and exaggerates them wonderfully. The picture is of blessing overtaking judgment. Before the farmers can harvest their crops, others come along and plant the next crop. Before the vineyard owners can process one season's grapes, the next season is ready to grow. Indeed, there's so much wine it flows down from the hills like a river. No doubt the quality of it would make the finest wines of the 21st century taste like vinegar. This is an unheard of, impossible, unprecedented plenty.

In these days there will no more talk of austerity in the news, and no more fears that bust will follow a boom. This peace and prosperity cannot come to an end. Not only is this a reversal of Israel's catastrophic destruction by Assyria in 722 BC, but it is a permanent state of affairs. Perhaps the best line in this promise is verse 15: 'I will plant Israel in their own land, *never again to be uprooted*' (my italics).

We need to know that this future is guaranteed to those trusting in Jesus Christ. We need to know that future prosperity is guaranteed in order to liberate us from a materialism that tries to accumulate wealth now. We need to know that God will bless us in ways never seen on this earth so that we don't try and build heaven now. Never, not once in the New Creation, will we ever think sacrifices made in this life were not worth it. We will enjoy our permanent home with our spectacularly generous God and be thrilled for all of the ways we have served Him in this life.

REFLECTION

Dwell upon this picture of the New Creation until you have a massive smile on your face and a song in your heart! How will this truth liberate you to serve the Lord today?

DAY 31

READ Amos 5:1–27 again

The book of Amos is a call to seek the Lord wholeheartedly. It's a call to trust in Him, not your own resources, nor your religious habits. It's a trust that is seen in a concern for justice and righteousness.

What changes would you like to make in your life?

Has your view of the Lord shifted a little?

He is the Almighty Lion who roars (1:2); He is the Creator of all that exists in this world (4:13); He is the One who ruins the strongest city in a flash (5:8); He is the One who touches the earth and it melts (9:5); and He is the One who will sieve and shake everyone who has ever lived (9:9).

Has your thankfulness for Jesus grown?

He is the One who was crushed for us; who gave His strength for us; who was stripped naked for us (2:13–15). He is the One who faced God's judgment on the Day of the LORD – a day when there was darkness at midday not light. He endured darkness when He only deserved light (5:18–20). He is the One who cries out and begs for us to be shown mercy, constantly interceding for us on the basis of His perfect life and that He's risen from an atoning death (7:1–6). He was the One who endured exile so that we can be planted in the New Creation forever (9:4, 15).

What will change in the way you 'seek the LORD'?

Have you been challenged about the place where you find security? Have you been made to think about why you go to church and how you honour the Lord there? What will it mean for you to let justice roll on like a river and righteousness be like a never failing stream?

REFLECTION

What resolutions will you make having read through the book of Amos?

An example to ponder

Back in chapter five we thought a lot about how 'to seek the Lord and Live' is paralleled with 'Seek good [justice] and live'. Many find it hard to effectively pursue justice and righteousness in this world while also maintaining the priority of sharing the gospel with unbelievers. One man I've found inspiring in his ability to hold these truths together is Lord Shaftesbury. In the 1830s his reform bills prevented children under 8 years old from working and dramatically limited the hours of 9–13 year olds. His schools educated 300,000 destitute children for free. He improved conditions in all British mental asylums.

But he also founded the YMCA in order to teach young men the gospel. He was President of the Bible Society that sent Bibles around the globe. He poured his fortune into supporting missionaries going to all the nations. He cared about eternal suffering.

Near death, Shaftesbury told his friend Edwin Hodder, 'My religious views are not very popular but they are the views that have sustained and comforted me all though my life. I think a man's religion, if it is worth anything, should enter into every sphere of life, and rule his conduct in every relation. I have always been – and, please God, always shall be – an evangelical.'

MORE IN THIS SERIES

ROMANS
Momentous News
By David Cook
ISBN: 978-1-906173-24-1

MARK
The Suffering Servant
By Jeremy McQuoid
ISBN: 978-1-906173-55-5

DANIEL
Far From Home
By Justin Mote
ISBN: 978-1-906173-68-5

1 THESSALONIANS
Living for Jesus
By Julia Marsden
ISBN: 978-1-906173-67-8

PHILIPPIANS
Press Towards the Goal
By Kay Mumford
ISBN: 978-1-909611-31-3

GALATIANS
The Life I Now Live
By Peter Mead
ISBN: 978-1-910587-09-6

ACTS
To the Ends of the Earth
By David Cook
ISBN: 978-1-909611-02-3

EZEKIEL
For His Glory
By Peter Lau
ISBN: 978-1-909611-83-2

JOHN
Never Thirst Again
By David Cook
ISBN: 978-1-909611-30-6

and more at... 10 Publishing
a division of 10 of those.com

To place an order call: **0330 2233 423** email: **sales@10ofthose.com**
or order online: **www.10ofthose.com**

10 Publishing
a division of 10 of those.com

10Publishing is the publishing house of **10ofThose**.
It is committed to producing quality Christian
resources that are biblical and accessible.

www.10ofthose.com is our online retail arm selling
thousands of quality books at discounted prices.

For information contact: **sales@10ofthose.com**
or check out our website: **www.10ofthose.com**